AF080434

Thunder in the Courtyard: Kajari Poems

poems by

Rajiv Mohabir

Finish Line Press
Georgetown, Kentucky

Thunder in the Courtyard:
Kajari Poems

Copyright © 2016 by Rajiv Mohabir
ISBN 978-1-944251-46-8 First Edition
All rights reserved under International and Pan-American Copyright Conventions.
No part of this book may be reproduced in any manner whatsoever without written permission from the publisher, except in the case of brief quotations embodied in critical articles and reviews.

ACKNOWLEDGMENTS

Editor: Christen Kincaid

Cover Art: "Megha Mallar Raga, Foloi from Ragamala *(Garland of Melodies)* LACMA M.71.1.24" is licensed under CC BY 2.0

Author Photo: Charmila Ajmera

Cover Design: Elizabeth Maines

Printed in the USA on acid-free paper.
Order online: www.finishinglinepress.com
　　　　　also available on amazon.com

Author inquiries and mail orders:
Finishing Line Press
P. O. Box 1626
Georgetown, Kentucky 40324
U. S. A.

Table of Contents

शुक्ला पक्ष
Bright Fortnight / 1

पूर्णिमा (Full Moon) / 16

कृष्णा पक्ष
Dark Fortnight / 17

अमावस्या (New Moon) / 32

for Jordan Andrew Miles

शुक्ला पक्ष
Bright Fortnight

Raga: मेघ मल्हार

समय: To be sung at night during the monsoon

Scale:

Ascending: S m R m P n S'

(मोर, कपोत, सांड, कपोत, कोयल, हाथी, मोर)

ताल: Jhap

प्रथम
●

आज पिया जायेगा विदेश
समन्दर मेरा नमक निगलेगा।

रे पानी की लहर,

मेरे किनारे से उसके किनारे तक
मेरी दुआ ले पहुँचाना।

Today my love leaves me;
the sea will drink my salt.

O wave,

from my shore to his
carry my du'a.

द्वितय
●

Sajana,

Wind shakes me   awake.

At midnight I call out
but my house
         is empty.

I clip my toenails past the bed,
even this body   is hollow.

The house is a metaphor
         for the body,
how literal must I be?

         Where is outside
where is inside?

     I call out   for you
but my house
       is empty.

तृतीय
●

Sajana,

I pluck a weeping cuckoo
                from the branch

and with one bite
        its breast   is a poisoned apple.

I pull feathers from my mouth,
                down sticking the throat.

Your song bleeds
        from my chest.

How can a monsoon bird
              prick the heart
              once swallowed?

What is this flutter
        against my ribs,

                this relentless sting?

चतुर्थी

A distant koyal
strikes one note
in three octaves.

  Piya.
    Piya.
      Piya.

पंचमी
●

Sajana,

You send a photo:
a plastic grey whale—
                a cetacean
that returns
      to California each summer.

From Waimea I imagine you
standing   on some Santa Barbara beach.
Your footprints
      fill with rain.

Radha drowns Krishna's prints
in her salt. His only sound
a ghost:
      his reed flute's blue wail.

षष्ठी

बिदेस से केसरवा भेजेला बलमवा
पिया तू ना जाने

केसरवा किसून के रंगवा
उही जे रधिया के छोड़ देले

जमुना के तीर भीगल गइल
तोहारे बाँसुरी के बेला से।

My love sends saffron from afar.
Piya, don't you know

saffron is Krishna's color,
the same Krishna who left Radha

on the Jamuna's banks, soaked
in the spell of your flute?

सप्तमी
(

Sajana,

After night's monsoon
the morning's silence unsettles.

Last night:
    your voice in symphony;
at dawn:
    a double bar.

Day's body is empty:
    all black notes lift from the staff

as swallows in heat. All instruments
refuse their strumming
    without hands

guiding rivers from their bells. I am
a flute with no one

    to press out
        my song.

अष्टमी
 ☽

Rain,
      do not kick up dust.

            O, dusk cloud,

Do not stir
      his memory.

नवमी
(

Sajana,

Apart,
    the ocean
        and sky pant

for the other's lips.

Clouds erupt
    from craving.

In the hot months
    your absence
        is like thirst:

so unmovable
    and yet so moving.

दशमी
(

Sajana,

Since you left
        I've not touched

your side of our bed,
    leaving   space

        for where you belong.

In a dream I hear
    your voice—

so soothing, yet
        stoking fire.

एकादशी
(

Sajana,

Come sunrise I regret
I can't pin my dream of you

on its back, and press my brow
into its nape nor drink

your body's scent before you wake:
that at dawn you are a shadow

                                            erased by light.

द्वादशी
(

झींगुर ने अपना कला शुरू कर लिया
नमी पार काट रहा है उसका गाना
कैसे काटूंगा समय पलंग पर लेटा
बिना तेरे?

झींगुर सिर्फ तेरा नाम जपता है
तेरी गीली याद से भला कैसे सूखा?
कोइ चौरा नहीं
तेरे नाम में डूबने छोड़कर।

The cricket begins his night-art,
his song cuts through humidity.

How to endure the night
                on this bed
without you?

He keeps chanting your name.
Soaked in you,
                how will I ever dry?

There is no other road
                but to drown.

त्रयोदशी
(

Raven wings, the cloud's
enveloping scale.

Moon orbs, emeralds on
the blades of grass.

Moist copper
incense: pine needles
in rain.

                                                  Humid dusk music.

                                                      Treefrogs, throats
                                                        swell dark hours,
                                                     long for the other.

                        In which month will you return?

चतुर्दशी

Sajana,

The sky and sea fuck.
This is why

        monsoons drive you mad;
the blood's salt burns hot.

On the shore, a sudden torrent.

Come back.

        Out this blaze.

पूर्णिमा
(Full Moon)

हम अभी अभी पयलिया बान्धे
अउर तू गहरी नदिया के पार गइला

महेंदी उतर जाये अउर तोहार
कोई भी निसनवा नाहीं रहे

I have just fastened my anklets
and you have crossed the deep river.

My mehendi fades and soon
no trace of you will remain.

कृष्णा पक्ष
Dark Fortnight

Raga: मेघ मल्हार

समय: To be sung at night during the monsoon

Scale:

अवरोहण: सा' निऽ प म रे सा रे ,निऽ सा

    (peacock, elephant, nightingale, dove, bull, dove, peacock)

ताल: Jhap

प्रथम

एगो कोकिला निगली ताकी
पिठवा से पंख उगाईहे अउर हम
बिरह के आसूँ पीअत है
इ नीमकहरमवा के
पता चलल कि चिड़िया नाहीं
हम सँपवा पालत रही
जिगरवा पर बैठके
पसलिया के पिंजरवा से
तोहार कजरिया सुनावत रहेला
इ कम्बख़्त कोयलिया

I swallowed a kokila so
wings would sprout from my back;
I gave it to drink anguish.
This traitorous thing
wasn't a bird at all,
come to find out.
This whole time
I had raised a snake
that sits on my heart
and sings from my breast
your *kajari*, your monsoon
songs,
this cursed bird.

द्वितय
)

Sajana,

Swells shadow-puppet
       dolphin shapes in the bay.

You are painted   on my sheets
the color of Krishna,   of illusion:
    the empty
        behind the shape;

a midnight storm head, your ruckus
refuses to let me sleep; the streak

of kohl on Radha's
       deserted cheek.

तृतीय
)

Sajana,

Bamboo shards float
    down
        every stream
            I cross.

As I walk   splinters stick
my feet,
    my palms,
        my eyes.

Somewhere inside
    your music
      will not stop—

will I never be rid of you?

चतुर्थी
)

The gully is a swollen river.

Rain overflows the temple pond.

rim
jhim

rim
jhim

rim
jhim

Drops are diamonds set in eye wells.

Piya, which road has swallowed your feet?

पंचमी

सतरंग के राम धनुसवा
    कहइलस जाइला
काहेकि सावन
    के महिनवा में

बिना तोहार
    बरसात का हर एगो
रिमझिम रिमझिम
    ख़तरनाक तीर

बन जाइला अउर
    इ बेसहारा दिल
सिकारी के निसान वाला
    भागत हिरण बनेला।

They call the rainbow
    "Ram's bow"
because in the month
    of Saavan,

without you,
    the rain's every
rim-jhim rim-jhim
    is a poisoned

arrow and this
    helpless heart
is a fleeing deer.

षषठी
)

Sajana,

Your imprint fills my heart
with dark,
   my throat
   with holes.

There's no need
   to take a flame
to hollow a reed, my bed
is sick   with night.

How useless
to be an opening, a thing
     of neither place.

What good is a reed
   without a shehenai?

How useless I am
   without you.

सप्तमी
◗

Sajana,

It took me years
        to realize
this body is a beena.

See the holes?   Here
is the hollow
        where your breath goes,

put your fingers   here to start
and stop   the flow.
        This

is where your lips
    are meant to go.
        That's why

the beena maker carved it.

अष्टमी

अब ना बजावो श्याम बाँसुरया
        तरसे लेगेला सावन के विरानिया

Krishna, do not play your flute;
        the loneliness of Saavan begins its ache.

नवमी

Sajana,

You're gone, so
    I threw away

every last reed
    I could find.

If I play this raga
    the monsoon will never end.

Why does the wooden lilt
    creep into my head

as blood
    circling my ear?

दशमी
●

Sajana,

I've taken to smashing flutes
with my hands and feet;

throwing them out won't do.
Some ghost finds them at night

and keeps me sweating in my sheets.

My friends now call me
Bamboo Smasher—

Imagine the panic in Kaneʻohe,
a town named "Bamboo Man"

when they hear you've gone.

एकादशी
●

Sajana,

Your ghost is a splinter
made from what I love:

      a trace of misery and music
that juts from my finger,

a shard of the flute
      I put to my lips:

      what once soothed the blood
but stirred the feet

now aches;
            now stabs.

द्वादशी
●

Wind shaken leaves,

                    melody swells

      twelve

            love stories

                  high.

Breeze—

                    do not play. Do not play.
                    Flute stream, do not flood.

त्रयोदशी
●

Sajana,

Like stars,   I string my tears
as pearls to count each
                    smooth star
in this constellation of want—

one hundred eight beads on the mala
strung with torn bedclothes.
                         Each bead

a bleary prayer,   each pearl an hour
spent without you,   each hour
a wraith   of your perfume.

Listless,
     my eyes are bloodshot.
When will you come to lend
                    an hour of relief?

चतुर्दशी
●

I am a raw vessel.

Play a beat on my clay lip:

>   *dhum dhum*
>
>   *dhum dhum*

>   Thunder in courtyard

> *dhum dhum*
>
>   *dhum dhum*

my body is this
un-fashioned earth.

Piya, come.
            Get your hands dirty.

अमावस्या
(New Moon)
●

सजनवा मारो ना नजरिया
तोहार अखिया के तीरवा से
ना हमार हिरदय तोड़ा

सुरहिया फ़टके भीगाई हमार वेस
बदनिया फ़टके हाँस उड़ जाई कउन देस

साइँया मारो ना नजरिया
तोहार अखिया के गोलिया से
जिउ हमार जड़ जाईहे

Sajana, don't look at me.
With your eyes
don't stick my heart.

My clay pot will break,
        soaking my clothes.

This body will break;
        no telling where
                this swan will fly.

Saiya, don't look at me so,
from your stare

            my life is lost.

CPSIA information can be obtained
at www.ICGtesting.com
Printed in the USA
LVHW042258270119
605466LV00001B/206/P